No Life After Death

Carl Crozier

No Life After Death

Carl Crozier

ISBN:9780998615226

carlcrozier10@gmail.com

Printed in the United States of America

BELLA JOHNS ENTERPRISES
Publishers

Introduction

I would like to live forever, as long as I could remain healthy and have no emotional or psychological problems. But I know that to live forever is impossible. Man must have known from the earliest of time that he could not exist forever. Death brings an end to life. It is not hard to think beyond life as we know it, to wonder if there is another existence waiting for the ending of life on earth to the beginning of another existence. It is hard to envision – THAT THIS IS ALL THERE IS? Once man was cognizant that death was life ending on earth, man attempted to substitute a live forever philosophy when they conceptualized the Life after death thinking, whereby humans would have another existence after their death on earth. Most men on earth have now bought into the life after death viewpoint, which has no way of being authenticated. We are told that you have to have faith that there is a life after death. Man found solace in creating the illusion of living another existence after death.

Living life to its fullest, staying alive as long as one can and enjoying their time on Earth are goals that every man does strive for.

Individual man is destined to live a very short time. If one lives to be 100 years old, that is considered to be a very long time to be alive. But it is a minuscule period in the time frame of the universe. The best that one can do in terms of staying alive on Earth is to try and avoid the pitfalls and complications that bring about death at an age earlier then the life expectancy for the group that should aspire to.

It is best that man take care of the existences that he has by avoiding the pitfalls of life shortening events that bring about early death such as: health problems, disease, accidents, murder, suicide, war, starvation, natural and manmade disasters. The above are some of the things that bring about life shortening events. Millions of men, throughout history have succumbed to not living a full life because their lives were cut short by one or more of the factors mentioned above.

As time progressed, man has gained knowledge about his environment which has allowed him to lessen the impact of those factors that prevented him from enjoying a whole life. Man's discovery of diseases, his creation of medicine to cure health problems and his ability to predict weather are some of the findings that have contributed to prolonging man's life. Man has relied on his own intellect to bring about the discoveries that have prolonged life. While living, man should continue to focus on moving forward life's accomplishments and avoiding life shortening events. Because as we now know it - and until - and if - life after death is proven, is nothing that can be done by man after he is dead.

Yet, some men, who have used their intelligence to make life better for themselves and their fellow men, have continued to spend time trying to convince themselves and all mankind that they will live on in some kind of spiritual world after they pass from their present life.

This book addresses that (1) there is no evidence for a life after death, (2) the many causes that rob man of a full life on earth which causes man's early death and (3) recommends that the real emphasis should be directed toward what man has been doing for ages. Discovering and handing down continued improvements in life conditions to prolong his present life and for the benefit of future generations.

Is There Evidence of Life After Death?

One of the most unsolved mysteries in life is death. Scholars and other learned people have been trying to ascertain whether there is life after death for ages. No one has been able to certify beyond a shadow of doubt that there is an afterlife.

As one approaches the age where death will occur, the thought of death will visit one more often. The crux of the mystery is "What if anything happens to the human existence after death? Is there life after death?" If we could all agree that there is no existence after death, then the mystery would be resolved. But most humans think that there is life after death. The majority of the population has some form of religious indoctrination which leads them to believe in some type of life after death. When those people who believe in life after death are asked "What do people do after death?" they do not have much of an answer. I was raised a Catholic and was taught that after death we will sit around and worship god if we go to heaven. The same religious teaching taught me if I had a bad life I will burn in hell – forever.

Many people believe that a dead person's spirit is still around after death and the spirit can influence things that happen in someone else life, who is still alive. I don't know how long that spirit is supposed to last or if there is a spirit. It is evident that most people cannot deal with the theory that all concepts of life are over after death occurs. I have not discovered any truth that concludes that there is life or any kind of existence after death. When I talk to people who believe in some form of life after death, they tell me that I have to have faith that there is this life after death. I am one that wishes that there were some kind of life after death. I have been lucky enough to enjoy my life, most of my life. I wish that I could live forever. That's not possible. I also wish that there could be another life after I am dead where I could be conscious of things around me and I could keep on enjoying the things that I enjoyed in life. I would even settle to enjoy new things that I now have no idea of. But, I do not believe that I will enjoy anything after death. I believe that after I die there is nothing else. I hope that I am wrong.

I believe that from the beginning of man's existence wherein he could rationalize, man has not been able to accept the proposition that there is no life after the life on earth has ended. There are three strong ides that man has attached to the end of life on earth:

1. Man goes to a paradise or a type of hell after death
2. Man is reincarnated into another life
3. Life is over and there is no other existence

There are certain things that human beings must do in a lifetime. One has to be birthed, breath, sleep, eat, eliminates, grow and age. Having Sex is not a necessary function in life. Catholic priest and nuns are supposedly celibate, and they make it through life without sex – so they say. But a sexual act is necessary for a human to be born. All of the aforementioned things are mostly considered as pleasurable and are necessary to maintain a normal life. Most people look forward to the operation of these basic life functions and will do what is necessary, within their means, for the continued operation of the factors vital for life. Humans will seek available health care when an intervention is needed to correct a basis function that has mal- functioned and is in danger of stopping one's life. The heart is the key to the body maintaining life. The heart pumps blood to all organs of the body and delivers the nourishments that are required in order for the body organs to thrive and function. Without a functioning heart, life cannot exist. There are instances when the heart has stopped for a very short period of time and then has been revived. Even though being revived, damage can occur to the body's organs. If the organ(s) were deprived of life sustaining blood pumped by the heart for an excessive period of time, that organ or organs can cease to function.

There is a phenomenon called Near Death Experience (NDE), It happens to some individuals who have been diagnosed as being dead because of no heart activity, but then they have been revived. Some of the people, who have been diagnosed as being dead, have reported that they have had an out of body experiences. I believe that I have had unexplained out of body experiences, that I could not rationalize - all of my life. When sleeping, I have had numerous dreams. I have flown in my dreams and did other thing that is impossible to do in real life. A reoccurring theme in my dreams is that I either misplace my car or it is stolen. It is my contention that the out of body experiences, experienced by near dead people are dreams that most if not all people have experienced. Man has been trying to interpret dreams since man's existence.

There are those who want to point to NDE as a proof that there is life after death, and they say that the person who has had that experience has gotten a preview of what happens after death. Again, my contention is that the person wasn't dead and that they were experiencing a dream.

There is one other function that humans and all living things experience that for the most part is viewed as non – pleasurable. That is Death. Except in the event that one commits suicide, or one grows too old and to infirmed to enjoy life, death for most people is unwanted. Death is a subject that humans think about or deal with only when they have to. Many people do not think about death until death comes knocking at their door. When a parent, relative or friend dies, one has to deal with a death situation. Occasional, when death is in the news, as in a mass shooting of innocent people, one's thoughts might engage the properties of death but for the exception of a person purchasing a life insurance policy and determining a beneficiary or making a will, man is too involved with life to be focused on thoughts of death.

Death by suicide might be considered as non-pleasurable. But the person who commits the act has found death more pleasurable or necessary then continued pain in life.

Death is the time in one's life when body functions cease to perform and one's life discontinues operating. Death is inevitable. IF you are lucky enough or even unlucky enough to be born, one will also die. Unlucky birth occurs when the person born cannot receive the basic nourishments – physical or mental- needed to grow and prosper, or the circumstances in which they are born ensures that they will have a miserable life – such as people who were born into slavery. Even people, who were born into slavery, got use to their condition and wished for life rather than death. They wanted to be free, but they did not wish for death.

In many cases, humans can extend the length of their life because of the invention of medicine and lifesaving procedures, but only for so long. Many people would like to live forever, as long as their body remains healthy. But everyone that is birthed is going to die. Whether we like it or not, death will see our mental functions cease operating and most likely our bodies will end up in a pine box, or in other means of disposal, if we die of what is called a natural death. Most individuals who die will be buried in the earth. Graves are dug in the ground 6 feet deep to house the corps. Burial at that depth prevented animals in ancient times from digging up and consuming the bodies. The burning of bodies called cremation has recently caught on as another way to dispose of bodies.

There are many ways that death can come to the human body such as: suicide, murder, accident, war, starvation, disease, natural disasters or natural causes. We will later examine the many causes of death and the way people die. Our objective in life is to live a life to its fulfillment and to hold off death for as long as we can.

Unfortunately, many people's lives are cut short for various reasons and they do not get to fully enjoy the contrasts of life.

Death remains as the biggest mystery in man's life. Religions have promoted the thought that there is life after death. Is there some kind of existence after life? The properties of Death have been speculated upon since man has been aware of his existence. I have thought about my own death and I think that when I die, it is over. Some people that I have talked to, speculate that death is a transition, going from one existence to another. No one can prove that theory and no one can disprove that there is No life after death. As we go further into this book let us see if we can examine death more closely to try and find anything that will indicate that there is a life after death.

Span of Life

The average life span of humans is 76.6 years in the United States. Woman in all countries of the world have a longer life expectancy then men[1]. The oldest person that I have known of lived to be just past 120 years. There is a story in the Bible where Noah, of Noah's Arch fame, lived to be over 600 years old. In light of known facts, I find the story of Noah's age to be a fairy tale, as I do many other biblical tales.

The country with the longest life span is Sweden, which has 80-year life span expectancy. All African countries have shorter life span expectancy then do most economically better off countries in the world. In the year 2000, a person in the African Country of Botswana had a life expectancy of 49 years.[2]

The life expectancy numbers have risen over the years as man has discovered medicines, procedures, cures and prevention of diseases. Man can also correct natural and manmade deformities that affect the quality and length of life. Medical discoveries such as antibodies, penicillin, vaccines, insulin, quinine, blood transfusions and hundreds of other medical breakthroughs have contributed to the preserving and lengthening of the life span of human beings. There

[1] "Life Expectancy," *Wikipedia*.
[2] *Ibid.*

was a time wherein, if you contacted cancer, you were given a short time to survive while the cancer continued to grow and destroy the body part affected. Today, there is a therapy (chemotherapy) that can be administered to a cancer patient that can stop the progression of the cancer cells depending on the type of cancer and when it is discovered in the body. Also, radiation therapy contributes to killing cancer cells. Cancer is no longer considered as an automatic death diagnosis. Medical research continues to discover methods to defeat cancer and other lethal diseases. Cancer still can and does bring about a number of deaths and is the second leading cause of deaths in the U.S. Only heart disease, which is the number one killer, causes more deaths than cancer.

Until recently, I had never given much thought of my own death. I have attended funerals of friends and relatives but attendance at those events did not ever trigger a rush of thought about my own demise. When you are young or relatively young and healthy, you don't have time to entertain thoughts of death. You are engrossed with thoughts of life and how to cope with the life you have before you. I have had some health problems while young which could have been serious but I will touch on those later.

Recently though, there were things that occurred which made me contemplate my own passing.

All of a sudden, I became aware of my age in relation to the span of a human's life in America. At 79 years old, I have already exceeded the average life span of an American which is 76.6 years and the average Life span of a Black man in America which is 71.4 years.[3] I then began to realize that each day I become closer to my day when I shall occupy a casket. Two years ago, my half-sister (from my mother) died. She was 78 years old and she died from cancer. At my present age, I have outlived her by 1 year.

Another incident that happened which made me more thoughtful of death occurred one day as I was driving my car to a destination. I pulled up to the corner of a major intersection in the south suburbs of Chicago. I was traveling in a southerly direction. The traffic light was red, so I stopped to obey the traffic signal. I looked to my right which was to the west of my position. I saw this vehicle with flashing red and blue lights approaching from the west. When I first saw the lights, I thought that it was an ambulance or some type of emergency vehicle. The vehicle was about a half block away from the intersection that I was trying to cross. As the vehicle approached closer to my intersection, I recognized that it was not an ambulance, but it was a long sleek black Cadillac

[3] *Ibid.*

hearse. At that point, I surmised that the hearse was leading a funeral procession.

I was in a hurry, as I seem to always be. I was about to become irritated because I knew that the funeral procession would go through my light when it would turn green. I would not be able to proceed on my way until the funeral procession had passed through the crossing.

I calmed down by thinking that the procession would only make me miss a light, but it was no big thing. I would be on my way after this short delay.

As the Cadillac hearse slowly went through the crossroad, I looked for the vehicles behind the hearse. To my surprise, I saw a flatbed truck with no engine which was being pulled by two beautiful horses that were in the hands of two men sitting on the flatbed truck. The flatbed truck was moving at a pace governed by the trotting of the horses. There was a casket in the middle of the flatbed. The procession was moving at a slow pace through this major thoroughfare.

'Wow', I thought. This is 2018 and I am seeing this type of funeral cortège that I had only seen in pictures depicting funerals with horse driven carriages before the invention of motor driven vehicles in the nineteenth century. There are pictures of Abraham

Lincoln's body being carried by a horse driven hearse upon his assignation in 1865. I had also seen pictures of other funerals in the time period before 1910 where a horse was the main mode of the corpse's transportation to the graveyard. I am a city boy, but it is still possible that they still use horses to transport the dead in the countryside. The thought also came to me that this could be some kind of ritual that was either religious or military.

Behind the hearse was a line of cars moving at a slow pace following the horse driven vehicle that took between fifteen to twenty minutes to clear the intersection. As I sat and watched the procession, I was amazed at the number of cars in the motorcade. I could not give an exact number of vehicles in the procession because when I started to count, a number of cars had already passed through the intersection. I counted over 100 cars from the time that I began the count.

I surmised that the dead person must have been a popular or important guy to attract that number of people in the funeral procession to the cemetery. I also know that everybody that goes to a funeral does not go to the grave site so there had to be others that showed up to this guy's funeral.

At that moment, as the cars finished going through the intersection, a thought came to me. Would I draw two cars when my body is transported to my grave? I'll be dead and will not know how I will be disposed of or who will come to my burial. Do I care? So why am I thinking about this?

I suddenly was no longer in a hurry. As I proceeded down the street, after I cleared the crossing, my mind switched from whatever I had been thinking about before my encounter with the funeral procession to the subject of death. I couldn't get it out of my mind for the next few days.

I speculated, most, if not all, who attended the service whose procession I had been watching, were evidently sad that the person no longer existed in life, with the possible exception that it was possible that some people were enthralled that the dead person is no longer around. Everybody is not loved by everyone. Some people wait, wish and hope for a person's death. Insurance money can be had. The living can be freed to marry another without going through the divorce procedures and there are those who while living can and have made life for others, what some would describe as a living hell. Those left behind are glad to see the departed go.

Unless you believe in the myth of the so-called soul rising out of the body and being able to survey all that is happening, you know the dead person, at that moment was unaware of the celebration being held in their honor. The view that dead people are unaware of things that happen after is a minority opinion.

People disagree with my assessment that the concept of the soul is an unproven myth. Still some other people and their religious organizations believe that man is reincarnated after death into the birth of another human being and that reincarnation will continue until the end of the world. Other people believe that there is a spirit that will leave the body upon death and will continue to float around on earth to influence the living. I wish that they could prove it.

Some others and religious organization have tried to make me believe, what the majority of people on earth believe, that some form of their being will leave the body (called the soul or spirit) and will go and reside in what they call heaven or hell. Those who believe in the theory of heaven or hell reserve heaven for men or women, who have led a good life, believed in their god and are forgiven by their god for the sins that they committed while in life on earth. Writers and artists have depicted heaven as a blissful place where those who have ascended to this mystical dwelling will exist in eternity.

Hell is a concept that is envisioned by many as a torturous, suffering place where those who have committed evil will reside in fire and brimstone - forever. Many artists have illustrated hell as a truly horrific place. Some religions postulate that those who go to hell will be there for eternity but there are other religions that indicate that hell is some form of a penal place and the soul will be released from hell after a period of time, like being in a hell penal institution.

I wonder what people and religions think of a baby who dies before they are old enough to commit sin or to do good deeds in the world. What do those people say about a baby that dies at 1 year of age or earlier? They die before they are old enough to do good or bad. Do the babies have spirits and where do those spirits go? I have never heard anyone tell me what would happen or where the so-called baby spirits end up. If I ask, they will probably have a rationalization for that question.

Since most of man's dead bodies are assigned to graves after their death and remain in those graves until they rot, we know that the body is not ascending to heaven or hell or the so-called afterlife. Therefore, man has invented the concept of the invisible spirit or the soul that leaves the body and is destined to exit the body after death. If that is so, then I guess that those that believe in the soul will espouse that the soul can experience pleasure or pain.

Getting back to the funeral procession, I surmised that the dead person in the procession that I viewed must have been a popular or important guy to attract the number of people in the funeral procession to the cemetery. Because of the number of people who were in the funeral procession, the dead person must have known while he was alive and healthy that his/her death would be celebrated to the extent that it was being celebrated. I wondered whether the dead person was expecting death or was it suddenly thrust upon him.

Who was the guy in the casket who was being celebrated in his death? Was he a young guy or an old guy? I didn't know why I thought of him as being a guy. I just took it for granted that he was a man. The corpse could have been a woman. What did the dead person do in life to make him so popular in death?

My mind continued to think of death for a few days after viewing the funeral procession. I began to ask myself questions about my own death. Did it matter whether my death would be celebrated when I passed? I answered by saying "No, it didn't matter". When I die, I am dead and no thoughts or awareness will I have after I am dead. The idea of death celebration is one that has been made for the living to think of. There are people who think 'Oh, when I die, they are going to celebrate my death. That makes me feel good now, while I am alive, to know that people will celebrate my death.' This is a thought that many will entertain while they are alive. My own thought is that I am not such a popular guy as the person that I saw on the hearse, so I will not have a throng of people attending my funeral. That's ok. I won't know about it anyway. There has been nothing in life that has impressed me to believe that there is any life after death or consciousness after one has exited life. Life after death has always been theorized by man as long as man has been able to rationalize life. There are many ideas and theories that man, since his history on earth, has been able to conceive that have been provable or unproven. Life after death is one of the one of the unproven ones.

Survival of Death Situations

I am lucky to be alive. I am glad to be alive. I survived birth and have so far persisted in a life full of uncertainties. All things considered I have had a good life. I was given up at birth because I was the product of an unwanted pregnancy. I was born at a time when abortion was against the law. Abortions could be had if one could find an abortionist and pay for the abortion procedure. Evidently, my Mother could not procure one or the other. So, I was birthed and then given up to the State to be raised. I have enjoyed most of my life and I have to continue to enjoy this life while I have it, despite the conditions that brought me into this world.

At the time that I saw the funeral procession I reflected on my life. My reflections then took me back to instances whereby I could have experienced an earlier death. Death could have visited me at an earlier date in my life more than a couple of times. I had some personal experiences with situations that could have brought on my death. After the encounter with the funeral procession, I would think back on those experiences, and will relate some of those occurrences that could have brought about a premature death to my being.

When I was about thirty, I was shot. Yeah - shot by a guy with a gun. The south side of Chicago is and always has been a place where many lives are lost to gun violence. I got into an argument with a guy in a bar and when I went outside to my car, the guy shot me in the stomach. I was able to drive myself to a hospital whereby the doctors operated and sewed me up. They left the bullet in me and to this day (49 years later) when I go through airport security. The bullet, which the surgeons left in, shows up. The doctors said the bullet didn't hit any vital organs, so they left it in. I didn't dodge the bullet, but I dodged death for the first time in my life.

I had a second encounter with a situation that had a potential to bring about my death. Once I was very sick and the doctors could not find the cause of my illness. I saw a number of specialists during this time. I was in my forties when this occurred. I was losing weight; my appetite was gone and I was lethargic. The physicians said that they had put me through all kinds of tests. Not knowing anything about medicine, I took their word that they had performed every possible test to try and find out what was wrong with me. They put me in the hospital while I continued to waste away was beginning to think that this was it. I am going to die. My doctor and an intern were assigned to care for me. The intern was right out of medical school. He had been on my case a couple of days when he told me that there was another test that he wanted to perform. He took some blood and the next day he came back and told me that I had syphilis. A treatment regimen was started, and I survived what was once a deadly disease.

Yet, there was another incident that threatened my life. If I would have been unlucky enough to have been born at an earlier time in life, let's say 1839 instead of 1939, I would have not reached my present age of 79. At the age of 50, I was diagnosed with prostate cancer. At that phase in my life, my doctor had been giving me testosterone hormone therapy injection to boost my sexuality. I had been regularly getting those injections because I was having problems with sexual performance. The injections worked.

At the same time that my doctor was giving me hormone injections, the doctor was checking my prostate by inserting his finger in my anus to feel my prostate. He explained why he was doing that procedure. I uncomfortably bent over the table and tolerated the intrusion into my butt as he performed the examination. He told me that he was keeping tabs on my prostrate because there was a chance that hormone therapy could lead to cancer. He asked me after he told me of the danger, if I wanted to discontinue the injections. I told him "hell no". The sex had never been better. He kept the shots coming every three months. This went on for approximately 3 years until one day the doctor informed me that he thought that I ought to have a biopsy. He indicated that he thought that he felt a growth in my prostate as his finger invaded my behind. He reminded me that he had told me that he had been keeping tabs on my prostate because there was a chance that the hormone therapy might lead to cancer. On the day that he informed me that I needed a biopsy, He alerted me that he felt that he had hit the cancer jack pot with his finger. I agreed to have the biopsy and the result of the test came back positive. I had cancer. I did not panic. I had faith that I could beat the cancer from the very start. At 50, when I was told that I had cancer, I didn't think that it was a death sentence. I remember that I did not have a negative feeling that the awareness of me having cancer affected my physic - negatively. I had faith in modern day medicine. I choose to have my prostate cut out of me rather than undergo medical therapy procedures. My prostate was cut out which eliminated the possibility of the cancer spreading. At that time, I was cancer free. They gave me an implant to replace the function of the prostrate which in my opinion was better than my prostate because I no longer had sexual performance problems. If you can believe it, that was one instance of cancer that led to a more enjoyable life. Over the next twenty-nine years of my life, because of the addition of the implant, which replaced the ineffective prostate, cancer caused me to have a more enjoyable sex life. The cost of the surgery and the implant, 50,000 dollars, was paid for by my insurance company. I no longer stressed about my sexual performance.

For the next Nineteen years after the prostate cancer, I lead a relatively healthy life, I reached 69 years old before I discovered a new health challenge/hazard to my body that presented a danger to my continued existence and again could have caused my demise at an age earlier then a normal life expectancy.

I do yard work around my house. I thought that I might have contacted poison ivy as I trimmed my bushes in the yard. I had an itching sensation in my breast that would not go away. I thought that I needed some kind of prescription ointment, so I went to my doctor. My doctor did a hand examination of my breast and then informed me that I needed to have a mammogram. "What" I said. Women have Mammograms. I'm a man. Men don't have mammograms". "You better have one" replied the doctor. I made an appointment to have a breast examination.

The technician that performed the examination grabbed my breast and clamped it into the mammogram machine. Men don't have much breast tissue, so the procedure hurt as the technician struggled to grab enough breasts to have the machine get a reading. When the results of the examination came back, it was positive. I had breast cancer. Having had cancer before, I did not stress about the diagnosis. My line of thought was to 'Ok, let's get on with the treatment.' My doctor made an appointment with the oncologist and upon seeing that specialist after he had gone through his tests and examinations, I was informed that I had second stage breast cancer. He informed me that my breast had to be cut off and I was going to undergo chemotherapy and radiation treatment to cure the cancer. I had no thought of death when I was informed of the malaise. I just wanted to get started with the treatment protocol. The only time that I can remember becoming concerned and or upset about my medical problem was when my doctor was having a problem scheduling the mastectomy. I knew that as long as the cancer was in the breast it could continue to grow. I was anxious to have the breast cut off so that the other treatments could start. It was almost two months between the discovery of the cancer and the time that the operation occurred. By the time that they cut off my breast, the cancer had spread to some lymph nodes under my left arm. After the operation my mind was at ease and I began a regiment of chemotherapy every three weeks for 6 months. After the Chemo treatment was over, I began radiation treatment for two months. I did not work while I underwent treatment. Fortunately, I had the kind of job that paid 70 % of my salary during the 8-month period while I underwent the treatment.

It's been 10 years since the onset of my breast cancer. 29 years since the prostate cancer. The thought of death never seriously entered my mind at the times that I encountered those medical problems. I understand that death anxiety can and does accompany some cancer prognosis in some people. Many people can and will die of the disease. But because of medical discoveries, the dreaded disease can be beaten, and death can be averted with the help of early discovery and medicine. I had a positive attitude when I discovered that I had cancer. A positive attitude did not cure me of cancer. I was fortunate enough to have my cancers discovered in its early stages, I received treatment and it worked to avert my early death, I had delayed my death to sometime in the future, I am going to die of something.

Life Shortening Causes of Death

There are many health related and other causes of death that bring about life shortening events. Earlier we discussed the fact that since there is no proof of a life after death then man owes it to himself to do whatever he can to live his life to the maximum of his life expectancy. Taking care of one's health to the extent that he can, is paramount to living a full life. Every person who is fortunate enough to be born ought to strive to live as long as possible to reap what benefits can be derived from their existence in this life – there is no other know life after their death that man can rely on. Getting the most out of the current existence ought to be man's goal in life.

Unfortunately, there are circumstances that happen in a life that individuals cannot control that have an effect on their quality of life and their length of time on earth. People who are born with bad genes that lead to health problems, that lead to early deaths have no control over that fate. They can seek health care and prolong life as long as possible, but health problems are the cause of many premature deaths. Throughout man's history, inroads have been made combating health care problems, but problems linked to health still account for a vast number of premature deaths of human. I deem an individual as dying prematurely when death comes before the age of the life expectancies of the individual. Life expectancies differ depending on where in the world a person lives.

One can be born in a country, at a time that the country is engaged in war or a conflict and as a civilian or soldier; your life can be ended early as a result of the discord.

Being struck by lightning or coming in contact with a live electrical wire can bring about an early death. There are many causes that can bring about an untimely end to a human's life. Some are nature's causes, others are manmade causes.

Since we have no proof of a life after death, we need to do all we can to eliminate or avoid those things that are detrimental to humans achieving a full productive life whereby they can contribute to the defeat of life shorting causes and pass their contributions down to the next generations.

There was a time when the average life expectancy was in the realm of forty to fifty years of age. Today, life expectancy is in the seventies because we have learned to combat and gain against the causes that cut life short.

Let's take a look at some of the causes such as: murder, health failures, accidents, natural disasters and manmade disasters that have robbed men of years of meaningful productive life. Man has lost millions of years of efficiency output over the ages because of early deaths caused by various calamities.

The following are the 10 most prevalent health related causes of death in America that come about because of health care problems.

Health Care Causes of Death

10 Leading Health Related Causes of Death in America[4]

1. The number one cause of death is *Heart Disease*. It is the leading cause of death among men and woman. Heart disease is a term used to describe several conditions, many which are related to plaque in the walls of the arteries. Life giving blood reaches the organs in the body by being transported through the arteries a blockage can cause death.
2. The second leading cause of death is *Cancer* which is a group of diseases characterized by the uncontrolled growth and spread of abnormal cells. The new growth of uncontrolled cells prevents the organ from performing its natural function. Lung cancer causes more death than any other cancer. There are many other kinds of cancer such as: breast, prostate, colon, rectum, skin; etc.

---

[4] Marcus, Mary Brophy. 2016. "The Top 10 Leading Causes of Death in the U.S." *CBS News*. June 30. www.cbsnews.com/news/the-leading-causes-of-death-in-the-us/

3. Chronic Lower Respiratory Disease occupies the third place in the cause of death of Americans. COPD is a collection of lung diseases that causes air flow blockage and breathing related issues.
4. *Accidents* are the fourth leading cause of death in the U.S. Vehicle collisions, poisoning, falls, fires, gun shots are some of the leading causes of accidental deaths. Accidental deaths are related to health care deaths in that accidents cause body functions to cease working.
5. The fifth leading cause of death in the U.S. is *Stroke*. Strokes occur when a weakened blood vessel ruptures. In general blood vessel ruptures in the brain are the main cause of strokes.
6. A disease that mainly affects older people, *Alzheimer's* occupies the 6th place in the causes of death among Americans. Dementia is an overall term for the disease. One type of dementia, vascular dementia, causes damage to nerve cells in the brain and affects the memory and ability to think clearly. People in the final stage are bed ridden; the cause of the condition is unknown. There is no known cure for dementia. It gets worst as time progresses.

7. The next leading cause of death which is the seventh leading cause of death is *Diabetes.* Diabetes is a disease where the body can no longer control the blood glucose. Persistently elevated blood glucose can cause damage to the body's tissues including the nerves, blood vessels and tissues in the eyes. Sugar build up in the blood can cause death.
8. *Influenza* and *Pneumonia* are in the eighth place among the leading causes of death in America. This disease has been around for a long time but still occupies a high place in the cause of death of Americans. It is caused by a highly contagious viral infection which is easily spread from person to person. Pneumonia can cause inflammation of the lungs.
9. *Kidney Disease occupies* the ninth place among causes of death in America. Blood passes through the kidney and the kidney filters the blood. If the kidney fails to filter and clean the blood the body will experience health problems which will lead to death.
10. Taking one's life which, *Suicide,* is the 10th leading cause of death in America. Hanging oneself, shooting and leaping off of tall

structures are some of the ways that people kill themselves. Depression is a major cause that can lead to suicide.

Of the above causes of death, health related issues that lead to death need to be singled out for some discussion. People, who die a natural death in old age, usually have a failure of one of their bodily systems. The human systems are built to last for so long. All human systems are not the same, in terms of the length of time that they will function. It is an individual thing. Some human's systems, such as: the heart, liver, lungs etc., are made to last longer than others and a system's length of functioning can be affected by the care or mistreatment that an individual provides to their systems. A person that abuses alcohol might expect that their liver will malfunction, and they might experience an early death.

I have included suicide and accidents in the above list of the 10 most causes of health-related deaths because suicide is considered a mental health issue and death from accidents usually involves some destruction to one's body system.

People that commit suicide know that they will be dead in, let's say, the next hour. What are one's thoughts if you know you are dying or will be dead in the next short period of time? Prisoners who are going to be executed are confronted with the circumstances that they know they are going to die.

History has informed us that some people who were executed left very moving statements when facing death. An American spy, who was captured during the Revolutionary War with England, was quoted to have said, "I only regret that I have but one life to lose for my country."[5] But he did not say anything about what he thought of death or the afterlife. Some convicts who have committed crimes, of let's say murder, apologize for their crimes.

Most people are religious and religious people have been taught that after they die, there is some kind of afterlife. Therefore, I suppose that those that are religious and about to die and they know it, they are taking stock of their life and are trying to figure out, whether they are going to the good or the bad afterlife. Good meaning to what they have conceived as good and bad meaning what those individuals have conceived as eternal damnation.

I would think that there is nobody who would think that they are going to hell. I suppose that those that have done wicked things against society, or another man and they believe in god, and believe in an

---

[5] Nathan Hale (6 June 1755-22 September 1776).

afterlife, they will ask forgiveness of the god that they believe in before they die.

There are times when we do get to know what the thoughts of dying persons are, if doing the process of death; they linger long enough to explain their thoughts. Some of us have had the experience of being at the bedside of a dying person and being privy to the thoughts of the person about to decease. I am sure that many family members have had that experience.

I had the experience of being with an individual who faced death and then recovered, and I was able to be privy to their contemplations about death during the process.

When a person is old, sickly, or injured, death can be an expected outcome for the affected individual. Some people recover from the condition that brought them into the near-death situation. But there are some circumstances whereby humans who thought they were going to die, made a dying statement, recovered and then experience unexpected instance death in situation where death was no longer contemplated by the victim. The following is a true story of one such individual's unexpected death.

Unexpected Death

Man has created many inventions and has utilized natural resources which have advanced civilization. The motor vehicle is one such invention. Although useful, the motor vehicle is an instrument of death. *Wikipedia* indicates that an average of 3,287 people die per day in automobile accidents around the world. I would surmise to say that most people who operate those vehicles are aware that an accident could occur which could take their lives. Because of that awareness, the vast majority of people who drive are conscious of the possibility of an auto accident and thus they drive safely in an effort to avoid collisions that kill or main.

Notwithstanding, statistics tell us that whether one is careful or not, accidents do happen and in many cases death will come about because of car and truck crashes. According to The World Health Organization, 1.24 million individuals will die each year because of automobile crashes. The source that provided that information does not indicate whether those that were counted in this death statistic died instantly or whether they died eventually as a result of the crash. If one lingers, before they die, as a result of a crash, then there is the possibility that they are aware of their pending death. Is it better to die instantly or is it better to know that you are dying and get to think about your death?

Recently, I had a friend who was full of life and loved to dance. She was a senior person who was retired but took a part time job to keep active. She was filled with the vigor of life. She danced every weekend at different dances given by senior social organizations. One day she was in an automobile accident on her away home from work. The police were chasing a car and the car ran into my friend's vehicle. My friend received considerable damage both to her vehicle and to her body. She was hospitalized to repair her broken leg and other parts of her body injured in the accident. After the accident, while undergoing medical procedures to try and save her life, my friend talked of her death. She was in pain and had to endure being hooked up to various devices that supported her injured body and pumped in life savings fluids. She was a person who believed in god and in an afterlife. When she could converse, she conveyed that she hoped that she had led a good life so she could be with what she called "her Lord."

The medical intervention that she received began to take effect. Eventually, the body props and the intravenous needles were withdrawn from her body. She recognized that she was getting better. She praised the lord for her recovery. I thanked medical science for the healing process that was taking place. I, being an atheist, could only be disbelieving of her faith in god. I shook my head in agreement with her statements about god and the afterlife. I didn't tell her that I disagreed with her assessment of the lord and afterlife. I wanted to be kind to her in what we thought were her last days in life.

Eventually, to everyone's surprise—including my friend—the medical intervention that she received took effect. The body was repaired enough to remove her from the hospital into a rehab facility. She had spent 6 weeks in the hospital, and she would spend another 5 weeks in rehab before she was well enough to be sent home. She was discharged from the rehab facility amid fanfare from friends and family. Her healing process continued at home. Her outlook for life was as bright as ever for this 73-year-old woman.

Two weeks later, after the rehab discharge, she had problems breathing and her son called for an ambulance. On the way back to the hospital, my friend died.

We were told that the cause of death was a blood clot in her lungs. She was a healthy person before the automobile accident. The auto accident and the operations that she went through changed the normal functions of her lungs which killed her. After her body began to show signs of her recovery, she ceased talking about an impending death. As far as she and her family and friends knew, she was going to heal and resume her life.

Death came to her. It delayed coming to her and for what reason nobody knows. To say the least, everybody was hurt. We thought that she had beat death. We felt cheated afterwards but as time passed, we realized the phenomena that we were opposing. Death is all powerful. I went to her funeral and heard the mourners praise her life and postulate that she was in heaven. I listened and did not contradict the heaven statements. I remained silent.

Man has encountered many mysteries in life. We have been able to solve many of those mysteries. We can prevent the birth of a human being through abortion or birth control. But we know that death is eventually going to arrive, it can't be stopped; it can only be delayed—sometimes. We don't know when its arrival time will be here. I am 79 years old. I don't know when death will arrive for me. But I know that it's coming. I have had a good time living, but I have no choice but to give it up when death comes for me. I have seen no evidence that there will be another life waiting for me after I die.

Deaths by Natural and Manmade Disasters

The earth provides man with natural resources to nourish his body. Some of those natural resources come under the heading of food. Food can cause man's death if it becomes contaminated but in general food does not cause the number of deaths produced by other natural resources. Water, wind and fire are natural resources that have throughout history contributed to countless number of human deaths. Nature has also provided other natural resources that are helpful to man but have affected the number of premature deaths experienced by man. Some of those resources are:

Oil	Coal
Lead	Copper
Uranium	Iron Ore
Tin	Silver
Gas	Electricity
Gold	Diamonds

The above minerals and natural resources are valuable to man. Since their discovery, man has found many uses for them to improve human life.

Besides death by old age or for health reason there are numerous humans that die each year by nature's disasters or from accidents that are tied to nature's natural resources. The above natural resources have to be mined, processed and turned into products that will help civilization and provide riches for those in control of the resources.

The mining and processing of the above have led to millions of deaths. These categories of death strike usually healthy people who have no awareness of their pending doom and bring about the early death of those affected by the event.

Mine Disasters

Numerous humans have been killed or experienced death by mine explosions while trying to process nature's gifts to man. Some of the fatalities are listed below:

Explosion	Year	Country	# Killed
Courriere	1906	France	1099
Senghenydd	1913	England	439
Farmington	1968	USA	78
Monogah	1907	USA	500
Soma	2014	Turkey	301
Benxiha	1942	China	1549

Because of all types of disasters and accidents, many people meet their end of life instantly without their expected knowledge of their demise. The following are a list of some of the disasters and accidents that have caused tremendous unexpected deaths among humankind:

Natural Disasters

Unexpected Deaths from Natural Causes

Deaths	Cause	Country	Year
500,000	Cyclone	Bangladesh	1970
300,000	Cyclone	India	1937
227,000	Tsunamis	India	2004
30,000	Earthquake	Italy	1915
25,675	Earthquake	Africa	1968
40,000	Earthquake	Portugal	1755
71,000	Volcano	Indonesia	1815
20,000	Explosion	China	1626
1760	Train wreck	Sri Lanka	2004
171,000	Dam Failure	China	1975
2,209	Flood	U.S.	1906
20,000	Theater Collapse	Italy	27 AD

The above are only a few of the disasters and catastrophes that have caused humans unexpected death during the history of the world. The list of all known occurrences could fill out many pages in this book. Many, if not most, of the people that were killed in disasters, their bodies were never recovered. Therefore, there was no individual funeral procession for those individuals. The country in which the disaster occurred might have held some kind of mass celebration or remembrance for the dead who perished in the event.

Man has improved and made advances in technology to try and predict natural disasters and prevent man made calamities. In countries where technology has advanced, the number of deaths from the above tragedies has been lowered. As an example, countries that have been able to build better structures have been able to lower their death statistics against earthquakes because the building that are built can now better withstand the destructive force of the shattering of the earth by earthquakes. Man is also now better able to detect nature's other destructive forces and can devise alert systems to warn the populace of coming destructive forces. Countries can build levees to control rivers, move man out of the path of hurricanes, tidal waves and volcanoes. But no amount of known technology will prevent all deaths by the forces of nature. The preventive measures have made some inroads into reducing death totals. But the forces of nature have taken millions of human lives and will continue to wreak havoc on mankind until and if man can completely control the forces that bring them about. Will we ever be able to totally control the wind, water, fire and the movement of the earth? I don't think so.

Invention Disasters

Besides the automobile which we discussed earlier, there are other inventions such as the airplane that benefited man, but the airplane has been involved in accidents that have caused fatalities and have taken a toll on man's life. These are a few of the airplane disasters:

Airplane Disasters

Date	Airlines	Deaths	Country
1977	Pan Am Flight	583	Spain
1985	Japan Airlines	520	Japan
1996	Saudi Arabia	349	India
1979	American Airlines	273	U.S.A.
1991	Nigeria Airlines	261	Saudi Arabia

Death by War

Since man has existed on the Earth, wars have been fought between groups of men. Wars are synonymous with death. Wars are fought for various reasons. They are fought to acquire land, wealth, power, security, conquest, religion etc.

War is a man-made disaster. Armies are mustered to fight the wars and men are going to die trying to kill each other. One of the results of war is the fact that mostly young men die. Young, strong, virile men who can withstand the rigors of war are drafted or volunteer to fight for their country. Their country involves their young men in some type of propaganda that instills within them an attitude wherein they do not mind giving their lives for their country or the cause that they have adopted.

Since the beginning of war, millions of men, if not billions, have been killed as a result of warfare. In the First World War, 1914-1918, 37 million people met their death as a result of that war. Wow, 37 million people met a pre-mature death and the world hardly blinked! In World War II, twice as many people met their death as a result of that later war.

Death by combat was not the only cause of people losing their lives or dying throughout the history of war.

War brought about unsanitary conditions on the battlefield. If soldiers did not die of direct combat, there was other circumstance that would cause death. In prior wars, millions died because of diseases which were spread as a result of the lack of hygiene in battlefield encampments.

The deadliest war in history in term of the cumulative deaths was World War II. From 1939 to 1945, 60 to 85 million deaths were calculated to have been caused by this global conflict.

In past wars, if a soldier did not die as a result of direct combat, there were circumstances that death would be caused by diseases that resulted from horrific unsanitary conditions or infections as a result of wounds received in combat. In today's wars, sanitary conditions have been improved and man has learned to deal with infections and wounds that once took the life of many soldiers. Many soldiers that would have been causalities in prior wars are saved as a result of man's increased ability to tend to soldiers that have received wounds in combat.

But despite man's ability to save wounded warriors, man has become more proficient in delivering death in war. Their proficiency in causing death in combat has replaced and out stripped the number of deaths that used to be caused by unsanitary conditions and infectious diseases. The invention of superior weapons has multiplied man's ability to spew death on and off the battlefield.

Around the time of the American Civil War, 1861, the Gatlin gun was invented. This weapon allowed the discharge of multiple bullets per minute to be discharged from a gun. Before this weapon was invented a soldier on the battlefield had to load one bullet at a time which took time before he could aim his rifle to dispatch an enemy soldier. The bayonet was used after the soldier unloaded his rifle into the enemy. About the same time that the Gatlin gun came to the battlefield the repeating rifle was also introduced to war. Soldiers could load more than one bullet at a time in his weapon and fire it a number of times before reloading. But the repeating rifle, although it was valuable, and improvements have been made to it over time, it was not the forerunner of one of the most efficient killing machines that ever made it to the battlefield.

By the time that the First World War was fought, from 1914-1918, The Gatlin gun had been upgraded to the machine gun. The Gatlin gun could fire 200-600 rounds per minute. The machine gun could spit out bullets at a many times greater rate of fire then its forerunner, the Gatlin gun. One man could control the rate of fire and mow down hundreds of men who would charge a position. During World War I, the tactics had not been altered to take in consideration the advancement of fire power. Officers sent troops pell-mell into the infantry position of their enemy. The machine guns mowed then down.

Military tactics at that time entailed massing a group of soldiers either on horseback or on foot to take a position. That tactic was tailor made for the success of the machine gun. The operator, of the weapon, sweeps the field and cuts down anything that moved. Can you imagine killing 500 men at one time? Those were the kind of numbers that were reported as a result of battlefield engagements that happened in 10 minutes of combat in World War I. Then in the next hour the officers would send in another unit to be slaughtered. It took years for the militaries to realize their stubbornness and that they had to change their approaches to combat in order to prevent the untold slaughter and deaths of their troops.

The invention of the machine gun greatly increased the fatalities of war, killing young men before their time on earth was due–was done.

During what was called the Great War (World War I) other devices to increase man's proficiency to kill and increase deaths were introduced. Gases had been invented that could be directed into the enemy line, if the wind was blowing in the right direction. Gases such as bromide, mustard, chlorine and phosgene were used. Gas attacks did cause fatalities, but their main effect was debilitating. It devastated the ability of the soldiers to continue to fight by blinding them or affecting their breathing efforts and their willingness to go across the battlefield.

The airplane used in warfare also increased the death proficiency of conflicts between nations. Not only was the airplane used to kill soldiers but bombs from the planes were also used against civilian populations. Havoc was caused by the planes in World War II that were designated as bombers. The German and the allied countries that fought against the Germans dropped tons of bombs on civilian populations in an effort to reduce morale by killing civilians, interfering with production and scaring countries into submission. The Germans firebombed English cities and Russian cities and the allied countries that fought against the Germans, firebombed the City of Dresden in Germany. The Americans used the same method to destroy cities in Japan. The estimated loss of the civilian population in Dresden Germany was 29,000.

That figure was produced by multiple air raids over the city.

The most prolific death caused by the dropping of a bomb was caused by the United States. In August 1945, The Americans dropped one bomb over the City of Hiroshima in Japan. It was a new type of weapon. An atomic bomb had been invented and which had explosive power beyond anything else that had ever been made and the bomb also had radioactive properties that kept on killing after the explosive power had dissipated. The bomb could kill thousands of people in one dropping and it did. It is estimated that 80,000 people died when the bomb was dropped on Hiroshima. Those people were killed on impact. Later thousands more died as a result of the victims being exposed to the radioactive properties of the bomb.

A few days after the Hiroshima bomb dropping, America dropped another atomic bomb on an additional Japanese city – Nagasaki. 40,000 deaths were experienced as a result of that bombing plus thousands more from radiation. The American strategy of causing the deaths of the civilian population of the Japanese Empire worked. Japan surrendered a few days after the last bomb was dropped.

After the Second World War was over and an assessment was made of the tremendous destruction and numbers of deaths caused by the dropping of the Atomic bombs, a number of countries got together and developed a Treaty on the Nonproliferation of Nuclear Weapons in 1968. The countries that had already developed the bomb pushed the smaller less developed countries into the treaty. The gist or aim of the treaty was to develop trust in the smaller countries that the countries with the bomb would act responsible and not use the bomb in future war fare. The countries that signed the treaty would stop producing bombs and ensure that countries without the bomb would only engage in nuclear development for peaceful purposes. Not all countries signed on to that treaty. North Korea, Pakistan and India did not participate in the signing of the treaty. Today those three countries have nuclear weapons. It is my estimation that in the future, other countries will disengage from the treaty and develop other kinds of weapons of mass destruction. Man's waring nature will not allow dictates from other countries to limit its ability to assert what it determines as its best interest. Those countries will assert its best interest through war fare if necessary.

Death by Combat

How do you send men into battle when those men know that many of them will not come back or that they will not survive the conflict? Those that are being sent have to know the odds are at least 50% that that they will be killed in combat. Earlier, I had said that countries employ propaganda and instill in its young men a sense of loyalty and patriotism. Scores of young men are of the mindset that they are ready to die for their country and scores have forfeited their lives to charge the enemy. Many, if not most that are on the receiving end of being charged, are willing to give up their live in the defense of their country or their cause.

There are some countries in the world where men can object to killing other men and claim that they are conscientious objectors of killing another man. In the countries where it is allowed, men who make the claim dodge combat. Countries that honor that claim are few. I cannot envision Russia or China during the Second World War honoring a conscientious objector claim. I can envision that those countries would throw a person who made such a claim in the front lines of combat.

Again, most young men who are in armies are willing to die for a cause. I don't think that they want to die but will except the action that leads to death if their country says it's necessary. It seems unhinged, from my perspective, but there are some men who will go to extra effort to put themselves in harm's way to achieve valor for their action that will end in their death. Throwing one's self on top of a hand grenade might win a medal but it also might bring about one's death. I ask myself, is there any cause that I will volunteer to sacrifice my life for?

I was in the army at eighteen. I joined the Army after high school because I could not find a job and I was not ready for college. Fortunately, for me, I joined the service when the country was between two wars. There was a truce in the Korean War which has lasted to this day. That war still has not ended, but there have been no recent battlefield deaths. The truce is between the North and the South Korean governments and since America was involved, it is tied to the truce. The truce started in 1954. I joined the Army in 1958. The Vietnam War did not start in earnest until about 1962 which is the year that I got out of the service. I did not face any combat situations where death would need to have been contemplated. So, death, did not cross my mind in the army, while I was in a relatively peaceful situation. At that age, my mind was on women and cheering for the time to pass quickly so that my 4-year enlistment period would pass. While in the Army, I developed the urge to go to college. The army cut my enlistment time to 3 and a half years, so I got out early. They did try and get me to reenlist. Fortunately, I had no mindset for further military life. If I would have reenlisted, they would have sent me to Vietnam and undoubtedly my body would have been in combat and I would have had to contemplate death.

America, unlike European countries has had a relatively limited number of deaths from war as compared to other countries around the world. The America Civil War produced the largest amount of deaths for American soldiers. The following is a list of deaths experienced by Americans in war:

Death of Americans in Wars

War	Deaths
Revolutionary War	4,435
War of 1812	2,260
Mexican War	13,283
Civil War	529,332
Spanish American War	2,446
World War I	116,516
World War II	405,393
Korea	54,246
Vietnam	56,480

Germany, Japan, Russia and England each suffered over a million casualties in World War II.

Indian Wars

There were deaths that were caused by wars of conquest that was fought by Europeans and their decedents on what turned out to be wars on American soil fought by Americans. Theses wars were fought against the indigenous people of America. The Indian Wars were a lengthy affair. The Indian Wars started on the land, which came to be on American soil around the middle of the 1600 hundreds and did not end until around 1923 with the defeat of the Indians in the Posey War in Utah against Ute and Paiute Indians.

The death toll of White men, Black men (buffalo soldiers) and Indians over a two-century period was never given an accurate total amount. The Indians won a few battles but lost the Wars. One of the most famous battles fought between the Americans and the Indians was the Battle at the Little Big Horn River where Colonel George Armstrong Custard's command, wiped out the Indians. The Indians were led by Chief Crazy Horse, a Sioux Indian.

In the end, the Indians were killed, beaten, displaced, starved and massacred into submission by the white Americans and their soldiers.

Wars around the world and in every century of man's existence have robbed many a human of their ability to lead a full and plentiful life and sent them to an early death.

Death by Murder

There are men and woman who cause death by murder. When one human purposely causes the life of another human to be taken, that could be classified as murder.

There are different kinds of murder. If an individual causes the death of another individual because the individual that caused the death was negligent, that is considered manslaughter. An example of manslaughter is when a person is driving drunk and causes the death of another person as a result of an accident caused by the drunken driver.

If two individuals are fighting and one individual is killed as a result of the fighting that would be considered as second-degree murder. The person that caused the death of the person that died did not have intent to kill the dead person.

If one person or a group of persons plotted the death of an individual and killed that individual, that by law is considered as first-degree murder. In this killing of the person, the killer or killers premeditated the prey's death. A husband plots to poison his wife and feeds her arsenic over a period of time which leads to her death. That would be considered as first-degree murder and the husband could receive life in prison or execution depending upon where the crime took place. The possibility exists that the husband could get away with the murder because many murder cases are not solved.

Many humans meet their death caused by murder before their lives are fulfilled. Humans have murdered each other since the beginning of their existence on earth. The reasons for murders are many. Murders occur because of hatred, jealously, greed, envy, revenge and sometimes at random because of mentally ill persons or stray bullets. Many, if not most of the people that commit murders are not apprehended. In Chicago, Illinois, over 500 people were murdered in 2018. Less than 16% of the murders ended in the capture and conviction of the person that caused the murder.

My brother in law was murdered. He was in his mid-thirties when he was shot and met his death. The murder happened 30 some years ago. He was from a family of eight siblings who were successful in their lives. Four had academic degrees and the other three had careers which caused them to be comfortable in their lives.

Kenneth (the brother in law) was also financially successful in the lifestyle that he chose but he chose an unlawful way to make his living. My brother in law chose the streets and the gangs to support his way of life. At one time he had a legitimate job but when he was laid off, he turned to the street creed.

Eventually he became involved in a criminal enterprise that is not so well known in the streets of Chicago. He became involved in dog fighting. Before he entered the endeavor, I didn't know that there was a dog fighting scene in Chicago. He told me about the enterprise and that he was making a good living at it. Most of the dog fighting occurred in Indiana where it was legal. He bought, raised, trained and fought Pit Bull dogs. I once visited him and saw his operation in a residential area on the South Side of Chicago. He had a house with a big back yard that was camouflaged by rows of large shrubs where he housed his dogs. There always were 4 or 5 pit bull dogs chained in his yard. Dog fighting was illegal in Chicago but like other illegal operations, dog fighting was a lucrative endeavor. He was making money and supported his family doing this thing.

Kenneth got into a beef with a fellow dog fighter over the ownership of some pit bull puppies. To the best of my knowledge the dispute lasted for quite some time. The other dog fighter was insistent that Kenneth pay him for the pups that he accused Kenneth of stealing. The two had prior altercations using fists to try and settle the dispute. One day the two were at a dog fighting event and Kenneth's adversary was carrying a gun. The two begin to argue and the other man pulled his gun and shot Kenneth in the head. Kenneth died instantly. The perpetrator was arrested and prosecuted He was convicted of second-degree murder. He did 12 years in jail and is now a free man and Kenneth is dead.

Some murder is weird. Here's one weird case:

Kyle Swenson, a reporter for the Washington Post reporter on a murder of a father by his two daughters in The *Sunday Tribune* of March 11, 2019. The father was 85 years old and suffered with dementia. The two daughters wanted to hurry his death. They wanted to sell his house and receive the proceeds. They gave their father a drink of alcohol spiked with sleeping pills. The alcohol diluted the sleeping pills, so the concoction didn't work. They then put a pillow over his face but that failed to kill him. The sisters next stuffed a rag down his throat, pinched his nose and held his arms down. That did the job. They killed him.

The sisters called the paramedics and told them that they had discovered their dad dead on the couch. The paramedics assumed that the elderly man died of natural causes. The sisters had gotten away with murder. They sold the house and divided the profits.

A couple of years passed, and the sisters made a mistake. The sisters met and romanced the same man. The sisters did not know that the same man was romancing both of them. One sister felt guilty about killing her father and begin telling her Romeo about the murder. He got her talking and recorded her on his phone. He was able to get the other sister talking about the murder and also recorded her on his phone. He took the recording to the police. The sisters were arrested and convicted of their father's murder. The policeman that caught the sisters said, "if they didn't run their mouth and confess to their lover, they would have never been caught." This was the case of an 85-year-old man, who despite his age, his death was before his time.

Other Murders

No mention of murder would be complete without the mentioning of the murder of captured and enslaved people by another group of people. Throughout the history of the world, whole or partial populations have been wiped out because stronger group of people hated, despised, or loathed another group of people. The murdering group of people advocated their intellectual superiority and viewed the effected group as an inferior people. Although world history has recorded many such incidents of murder by one group of another, two incidents stand out in my mind.

African people were captured and enslaved by white Europeans and by Americans. Through three centuries, starting in the 1600 hundreds, Africans and their descendants met their death by murder by being thrown into the sea while being transported to America for the purpose of being slaves and by being lynched after coming to America. Even after the slave population gained their freedom in 1865. They continued to be lynched by Whites for another century. The murderous culprits never paid for their crimes.

During the Second World War, the country of Germany and its Allies tried to wipe the Jewish population from the face of the earth by murder. It is estimated that 3 million Jews were killed by elements of the German government, their army and their sympathizers between 1939 and 1945. A history of hate for the Jewish religion by Christians and other perceived Jewish faults fueled this lethal behavior by Germany toward the Jew. The Jews were shot, starved, worked and gassed to death. A few Germans were convicted for war crimes at the end of the conflict.

The Process of Death

Death starts with the beginning of life. Every person that is born begins a life cycle that will eventually take them to death. One's life can be divided into cycles. I have identified four cycles that can be associated with a person's life. Others might identify more cycles and others might have different opinions of what happens in the cycles of life. The following are life cycles and occurrences within those cycles that I have identified.

Human Growth Cycle #1

The human growth cycle starts when man is born. At the beginning of the cycle, the body and the mind experience growth. All organs of the body start the growth process. A baby who might have weighed 6 pounds at birth will have gained considerable weight by the time the infant reaches two years of age. Not only does the physical growth commence at birth but the cognitive process starts immediately. The growth of the brain enables the child to learn. Initially, learning is achieved and displayed by imitation. The child learns to associate actions with language and can respond to request and commands by imitating the actions of others. This growth process continues and becomes more sophisticated as the child grows. Muscle, bones and brain capacity develops. This cycle of growth continues until or about the age of 18. In some instances, the body growth outpaces the reasoning process of the brain. A teenager who looks to have a fully developed body may not be mentally fully developed. The body development can achieve maturity for some individuals in their mid-teens. By the age of 18 the person should be ready to progress to the next growth cycle.

Human Growth Cycle #2

At about the age of 18, man proceeds to the next growth cycle. The body is near completion in development by this time, but the brain also has developed a competence for learning. The individual uses what was learned in the first stage of brain development and adds to its knowledge base as its capacity for learning continues to receive input from its surroundings. The brain receives input to help the individual comprehend how to adjust to conditions of life. Such as: a job, additional education, social interactions and the acceptable cultural behavior. This cycle lasts until the early forties when the body begins the process of starting to breakdown. This start of the body breakdown can be readily seen in athletes. Many professional athletes retire from their endeavors in their mid-thirties. It is exceptional to see an athlete continue to be active into their forties. The muscles and the bones in the body have ended the period of their greatest use. The brain, in this period, which was developed from the first cycle, has been ready for input so that its capacity can be fulfilled. The brain capacity can lay dormant if it does not receive the input needed to function at its maximum. An example of this would be that the brain is ready to develop input into scientific exploration but if it receives no input from the owner of the brain, it will lay dormant for science inquiry.

<u>Human Growth Cycle #3</u>

In my estimation, growth cycle number three lasts from the mid- forties until 65 or nowadays 70 years of age. Most people know that the body is no longer what it used to be. Many people will start experiencing aches and pains in this stage or cycle. It is the goal of people in this category to prevent the accelerated breakdown that can happen if one neglects the body. But there are also people in this category who feel no change as they continue to enjoy the life that nature gave them, but as one progresses through this stage, the body undergoes changes. Many people put on weight which occurs because the body does not process food like it used to. Medicines are taken to keep the body organs functioning the way nature intended them to function. And as one advances through this stage the energy level that use to be there dissipates. The brain, early in this stage, should be operating at maximum capacity depending on what input has been fed into it during earlier times. At the end of this stage there can be the lessening of brain power depending upon the rate of brain deprecation caused by disease such as Alzheimer's.

Human Growth Cycle #4

The last stage in the cycle of a human being's life will lead to their death. Death can come at varying ages during this cycle. I have known people to live to be 120 years old. Remember, what we earlier learned that the average life of an American is 79.6 years of age.

At this stage in the life cycle, the body gives visible signs that it is deteriorating. The skin develops lines and wrinkles. As one grows older in this cycle, there will be problems with bones and joints. There is a change in the body organs such as the bladder, the stomach, the heart, the kidneys and other vital parts of the body. At this stage, consultation with physicians and the use of prescription medication might enable the body to maintain a near normal lifestyle.

The brain also shows signs of deteriorating during this period. Forgetfulness during this stage is a sign of the brain losing its function.

Death will end this stage in the cycle of life. Some deaths occur instantly, and other humans slowly deteriorate and end life in some type of medical care.

The above cycles of life and what happens during those cycles are my estimation of what happens from witnessing the lives of others and my own life. I understand that occurrences happen at different times for different people. I know two people who are able to run the marathons at 75 and 77 years of age. I would drop dead at the finish line if I tried such an endeavor at 80 years of age.

In general, though, I think my estimation of what happens in the life cycles of humans is accurate.

Death by Suicide

In the nineteen twenties and thirties, a number of people in America committed suicide as a result of losing their financial position that they owned in the American Stock Market. People purchase into ownership of companies, buy buying into the company's value through stock purchases. When companies loose value, the people who bought into the company lose their money.

In the late 1920s the stock market crash had a tremendous effect on the finances of America. The stocks and bonds, which represented money and finances, tremendously lost value and the many investors and owners of those commodities ended up broke. Individuals lost millions of dollars because of the failure of the stock market. Not only did Wall Street collapse but the country's banking system was affected by the Wall Street failure. The collapse of Wall Street sparked a run on the countries banks and people were lined up to withdraw their money from the banks. They had lost trust in the banking system. Depositors wanted to get their cash out of the banks. Because many people demanded their money at the same time, the banks depleted their stock of money. The banks were also invested in the stock market with the depositors' cash. When Wall Street failed, the banks lost the depositors' money. Banks closed because they ran out of money and they had lost their account holders funds. The banks were not insured by the federal government as they are today. Today, if a bank fails, the depositor money is insured to an amount of 200,000 dollars. The Federal Government will protect the depositor to the aforementioned amount. Back in the time of the Wall Street collapse, if the bank went under, the depositor also went broke. He lost his money.

Some people who lost their money could see no other way out but to commit suicide. They had invested their future in the money that had been committed to the market. They were smug in the thought that their life was without financial problems for the rest of their lives. Once they had lost their future, some jumped to their death from tall buildings and others utilized other methods to bring about their death. Evidently those people who brought about their own death because of their financial crumple did not think that they could recover and did not believe that there were other options that they could engage in to rebuild a successful life. Therein they took their lives.

Psychologists say that mental disorders, personality disorders, bipolar disorders, depression and substance abuse are risk factors for suicide. I bow to the professional opinion as to why people commit suicide.

In the suicide cases connected to the Wall Street crash. I think that depression was the factor that caused people to choose death over continued life. The loss of money will cause depression. The loss of a job will cause depression. The loss of a love one or of love can cause depression. I can see if you lose something that is so valuable to you in life and you don't see a way of recovering that lose, you might be driven to contemplate suicide and prevent yourself from living a full life.

There was a time in my life when I might have considered suicide if I had not been able to identify an option to overcome a situation that led me to a deep depression. I lost a job when I was in my mid-thirties.

By the time of my early thirties, I had worked hard during my early years to attain good fortune in life.

Coming from a beginning of being an orphan, being raised in foster care and a boys' home, I was able to attend college, receive a master's degree and progress up the job ladder. After graduation, over a period of time, I went from new recruit, to supervisor, to manager at various organizations. Eventually, I became Executive Director of an organization by the time I was in my mid-thirties. Then I made a stupid mistake.

I worked as Executive Director for an organization that accepted toys to give away at Christmas time. I took two of the toys for my own son. I got caught taking the toys. I had to resign. I was so embarrassed. I had let down all of the people who were proud of my accomplishments. I did not want to face anybody. I hid in my room for days. Thoughts of ending my life surfaced. Then a thought came to me. I could run away. I had money. I picked out a city on a map and determined that I was going to Baltimore, Maryland, because Baltimore had a large Black population. Maybe I could rebuild my career in that city. I packed my things in my car and one day while my wife was at work, I left Chicago and my home.

I drove to Baltimore and got a job as a security guard. The urban League which is a Black organization that assists its people with jobs and housing, among other things, helped me to find a job with one of the best hospitals in the country, John Hopkins Hospital. It was during the time of affirmative action and White businesses were looking to hire Blacks as a way to make up for past discrimination. I was hired as a labor relations specialist of which I had a background in. After I was there for six months, I reconnected with my family. I stayed in Baltimore for two years to rebuild my career. I then resigned and came back to

Chicago and I was able to continue my career-successfully.

Everybody can't run away from their problems, but one has to think of options when confronted with life changing situations. I don't know what I would have done if I didn't have that money to rebuild another life.

I also think that guilt can drive one to suicide. There are a good number of policemen who take their lives. I have an opinion as to why they take their life. My opinion is not backed by empirical evidence. The only evidence that I have is from experiences in my youth. I believe that cops take their lives because of the mean and evil things that they do to the people in the communities that they serve. I have witnessed numerous beatings administered to Black people by both white and black police officers. It is my theory that sometimes guilt catches up with those officers and they take their lives.

The Afterlife Based Upon Faith–Not Proof

In prior chapters, I have examined the many ways that death can stop a human's existence in life. I also hoped to try and answer the question 'is there anything or any kind of life after death' which so many people believe in.

I did not discover any new facts that would lead me to believe that there is some sort of after death life. I acknowledged that the thought of an afterlife has been hypothesized by religious groups and most people on earth have bought into that concept and believe that they will continue in some form of existence after their life on earth is over. It has been ingrained in most religious followers, no matter what the religion, that man somehow has a life after death. The people who believe in the continued existence of an after death condition cannot present evidence of their belief but they use the adjective that is used for most religious beliefs: "I have faith that there is such a thing as Life after death". Faith has been ingrained in religious followers, no matter what the religions is, to postulate the word "Faith" when the thing they believe in is beyond reasoning or proof. Faith is also used in the commercial world by entrepreneurs "have faith in my product," so they say.

Faith is asked by religious followers to have complete trust, belief, confidence, reliance in someone or something because religions say it is so. The way that faith is being defined here is that it is trust without evidence of performance or existence. A thing of faith has to be tested for truth.

We have come to accept what is called the scientific way. A thing is tested over and over again before it is accepted as a truth. Things that are true have to be verifiable. Life after death cannot stand the test of being verified. The concept of heaven or hell cannot be verified, which are so called after death places that humans are supposed to reside in, after they have passed from the earth. There is no test for reincarnation that has stood the test of time that I know of.

I think that there is a place in our existence for the word 'faith.' The word faith can also be defined as being based upon something in our experience or experiences. Some of us can believe in having faith in our ability to transport by air to different places in the world. That faith is based upon the performance of aircraft. The air transport system has transported billions of people around the word for over 50 years. Occasionally, there is an accident and planes crash but that does not deter people's faith in air travel. People who have never been on a plane will hop on the next plane leaving and go to their destination because they know the airline industry's record of safety and they have testament from other people who have flown. People are willing to test the odds that they will not be the next death statistic from a crash. Experience and knowledge of others' experiences gives them faith.

Experience can also cause one to not have faith in an entity. I see that many people lose their money in the casino Industry. I don't need to experience a personal lose. I can look at other peoples' experience and determine that I don't have faith in my ability to win a lot of money playing poker or other gambling games. Although some people win, I have no faith in playing games of chance.

There are many religious doctrines about faith. One such doctrine states that a follower should have a strong belief in god or in the doctrine of a religion based on spiritual confidence rather than proof. Most things in religion cannot be proved. Let's look at a few beliefs as an example of dogma that cannot be proved. The few doctrines that I have pick out deal with death.

1. Reincarnation—Numerous religions, especially the Hindus, believe that after one dies, they

will be reincarnated into another being. It can't be proved –Its based upon faith.

2. Holy Communion—Catholics believe that when the priest serves bread and wine to their faithful at their weekly celebration of mass, that the faithful are receiving the body and blood of the son of their god, Jesus Christ who was put to death. It can't be proved that this food and drink are the body and blood of anybody. The belief is based upon faith.
3. Most religions believe in a life after death in that there is a spirit or a soul that rises from the body and this entity resides in what they call heaven or hell. Where this entity goes, according to the religion, depends upon the human's behavior while he/she was alive. It can't be proved. This dogma is based upon faith.

There are many religious beliefs about death and an afterlife that the followers of different sects accept as truths based upon their faith in the ideology of the creed that they follow.

Some men have invested energy and thought in trying to make a determination about death or solving the mystery of what happens to our beings after we die. But I really think that most people don't stress or invest a lot of time thinking about death. They accept what their religious leaders tell them about death and move on with their life. Only when they are confronted with a death situation do they really think about death. If thoughts about death were constantly on one's mind it might make one appear a little ghoulish. I do admit that nevertheless, unless a person experiences instant death, there will be a time when everyone will contemplate their own death.

Life after death is a key factor in religious belief. Religions are always talking about death and the thereafter. The religious faithful (as do all men) spend a fixed amount of time on earth. They are told that they will spend an eternity in an afterlife. But some inquiring minds want to know, what is death all about, if there is such a thing as life after death? What kind of life will I have after I pass on from my present life? I don't blame them for that investment of time trying to solve the mystery of death. After all, we have been on earth for 50, 60, 70, 80 years or more and it is hard for most men to think that it will end, just like that without knowing what is ahead for us after we die, if in fact we believe in life after death. Man has been programmed by other men to think that there is something else after life, but no one can demonstrate what it is like.

I, like most human beings, have gone through the process of wondering what will happen to me after I die. I don't know. Writing this book didn't get me any closer to knowing what if anything is in store for me after I die. There is nothing that I have experienced in life that makes me believe in a life after death. I do believe that all the pundits and so-called religious men who have written about and talked about death and have espoused the theory that there is an afterlife are guessing. But I believe that they truly believe in the theory that they put forward without any unequivocal proof that there is an afterlife. They have trained their mind to believe in the concept.

Throughout the history of man (except in ancient religions) there have been only a very few claims that I have known, whereby someone has reappeared after their death and made a statement indicating that they once lived. In the ancient histories, with their ancient gods man and gods were always jumping in and out of reality. In the modern Christian religion, their god and savior, Jesus Christ, was supposed to have risen from the dead and appeared to his people. It is claimed in the Christian holy book, the Bible that this happened. Mary, his mother, was also said to have appeared and was purported to have been seen centuries after her death. Her appearance was said to have happened twice in France: once to a woman warrior, Joan of Arc and another time to a peasant girl at Fatima. There is no compelling evidence that those appearances happened but that they are part of religious myths that all religions use to tie their followers to mystical events. There might be other religions, besides the Christian, whose persons of religious relevance has been purported to have appeared after death, but I am not privy to those claims, if they exist. I cite religion in this part of the discussion because life after death is a religious concept not a scientific hypothesis. I find nothing to support the claim that there is life after death. I do find that life before death is what should be the focus of the human study.

Life Before Death

In my estimation what is important to humans is life before death. I am confident that most people agree with that statement. There is no creditable evidence that anything happens to humans after we die. What we do before we die is something that we can control and have some understanding of. As time passes, throughout the history of man, we have been able to solve things that prior generations of our ancestors were unable to solve. But those prior ancestors worked on the problems and handed down partial solutions, actions and behaviors to generations which came after them. Later generations carried on the research and completed answers to questions that had been raised in prior generations.

We all had ancestors, whether we knew those ancestors or not. Many of us knew our grandparent(s); some of us knew our great grandparent(s). But there were thousands of generations before us who we have no idea of who they were. Those generations had an impact on our present lives. The prosperity we have as a world is associated with our forefathers.

I can take my thoughts back a few centuries to the 1600s, 1700s or 1800s. My ancestor had to arrive in America as a slave during one of those periods. That ancestor could have been a man or a woman. There were other ancestors who were in Africa before the ancestor who arrived here as a slave. I, like every other Black person in America could go back and back in thought to trace our ancestors who were in Africa before the ones that were transported to America. We know that blood lines are handed down. This is not a myth. We know that ancestry is real. For the most part we just don't know who they were.

The average person may be able to tract their linage back two or three generations. One probably (might) have known their grandparents and maybe their great-grandparents. Families that trace their lineage can get to know names and maybe pictures of ancestors. But there is a point in time when the ancestors are untraceable. Untraceable ancestors did exist.

I also probably have European ancestry. I am brown skin in color, and I saw a picture of my great grandmother and she looked white. The picture that I saw was taken in the early 1900s. America is full of Black people with mixed completions that mainly resulted from White people taking advantage of Black women sexually. So many of our Black people have mixed ancestry, but we don't want to try and examine racial mixing now. That is a discussion for another time. The point is that we have inherited traits from those that went before us and the world population has thrived on hand me down heritage from ancestry millions of years ago.

The important thing is to acknowledge that those ancestors, thousands maybe millions of years ago, started our blood lines and handed down what we call legacies and heritage to us and to the world populations. Scientists estimate that man has been on earth in one form or another for 65 million years. It's a proven fact that generation after generation handed down to future generations vestiges that could be built upon to advance human civilization.

Men invented tools that assisted them in handling tasks for survival. Man discovered that there was a use for fire. We could cook our food. Another generation learned to cultivate the fields for farming so that man could stay in one place and did not have to follow the animals for survival. As generations developed skills, they passed them on to those that followed them. The generations that inherited skills, took them, improved them and passed them on to those that came behind them. In the context that I am writing about, it might have taken generations thousands of years to develop improvements for the conditions of humans. But man stayed true to their task of handing down what they inherited from the previous generation to the generation that came behind them. Men also worked to improve their inheritance. Those prior generations made improvements so that man could move things easier with the invention of the wheel, sail the oceans, read and understand the stars and spurred on future generation to continue to improve man's condition on earth.

Man inherits heritage. Heritage is the full range of our inherited traditions, cultures, values, laws, behavior, objects, and monuments that have been handed down and are still valuable to man, generation after generation. Most important is the full range of contemporary activities, meanings and behaviors which have been passed down throughout the ages. The good or wickedness that civilization has is associated with our forefathers.

Everything that our forefathers did was not good for civilization. Some of our forefather's actions were detrimental to the existence for their contemporaries and for future generations. A number of our forefathers who had control, murdered, raped and set conditions for their fellow man that were less conducive for a satisfactory life for those whom they controlled. As is the case today, our forefather generations contained the good and the bad as far as legacies are concerned. The world's ancestries contain the names of many such men who were detrimental to their own generations. The following are the names of a few of those men:

Emperor Nero—AD 37-67

Burned to death followers for public display, of the new Christianity religion – had his mother put to death.

Slave Masters

Throughout world history, there was countless number of people(s) who robbed people of their lives by enslaving and putting them to death.

Pol Pot—1925-1998

He led the Communist party (Khmer Rouge) in Cambodia. Pol Pot forced citizens into slave labor and murdered over 2 million people whom he deemed enemies of the communist philosophy.

Adolph Hitler—1889-1945

Chancellor of Germany from 1933 to 1945. Hitler ordered millions of people to be put to death based upon their religious beliefs.

Ivan the Terrible—1530-1584

Ivan the Terrible was Tsar (ruler) of Russia. He transformed Russia from a small country into an empire at a cost. Ivan violently purged the Russian nobility to gain control of the country.

Idi Amin—1925-2003

Amin ruled Uganda in Africa and persecuted ethnic and political groups to gain control of the country in Africa. International groups estimate that between 100,000-500,000 people were killed under his regime.

Joseph Stalin—1887-1953

Under Joseph Stalin, the Soviet Union (Russia) was transformed from a peasant society into an industrial and military superpower. He ruled in terror and millions of citizens died as a result of his brutal reign.

Leopold II—1835-1909

He was King of Belgium. As king of Belgium he, conquered and enslaved the people of the Congo, a Country in Africa. He ran the Congo for his personal enrichment. He enriched himself by forced labor from the native population. His Congo administration included murder, torture and other atrocities.

There were many more individuals and their followers who existed in prior generations throughout the world in many cultures, whose behavior was injurious to civilization at the time of their influence upon the World. Many cultures had evil forbearers whose bad behavior had to be overcome by generations that came after them.

Fortunately for civilization, generations that came after those men who caused the world's misery, were able to overcome the sadistic behavior and continue to advance man toward achieving knowledge and harmony in the world. Thank goodness, the good people who came along after the bad did things to overcome the malicious behavior of some of the world's evil forbearers. They undid the horrible things done by the malicious people in generations before them.

When we reach the age of reasoning, we as individuals need to be aware that we are creating a legacy from which those that come behind us can look to value what they inherit from us. They can carry on the legacy and build upon it and leave it, after they pass on. In the world, cultures leave values and knowledge those future generations can build upon.

In some families, riches in the form of money and property are left to future generations. Each individual must be aware that what they do will impact those that come behind them. I am sure that many individuals around the world are aware of some of the things that their mothers and fathers and grandparents did to improve their lives.

In my own family, I can cite a happening that occurred before I was born which undoubtedly contributed to the betterment of my life.

I was not raised by my mother. I was raised in foster care, but I knew my mother and my grandparents. My Grandfather did a thing that was instrumental in my life before I was born. He migrated from Alabama to Chicago in the late 1920s. He came to Chicago during what was called The Great Migration of Blacks coming to the North in that era from the South. He along with other Black men, were looking to economically better their lives. There were jobs in the North in industry that would hire Blacks and pay them a livable salary. That was the attraction. My grandfather brought his daughter, my mother with him. My Grandfather found in the North what he was looking for. He found employment - that he would have been unable to find if he had remained in Alabama. He was hired by the railroads as a Pullman porter. That was an excellent job for a Black man at that time. He was able to save his money and buy property after he had been in the North for a period of time. He was able to accumulate wealth.

Now, his good fortune did not affect me personally. I never received any support from him or inheritance from him after he died. I did not benefit from the family's good fortune while he was alive. Nor did I receive any of the benefits from the income that he and my mother eventually made. To the contrary, when I was born, I was kicked out of the family. When pregnant with me, my mother contacted TB. I am not totally sure why, but the family decided to give me up to the State to take care of. I became a ward of the State of Illinois and lived in foster care until I was 13 years old. Then, I was sent to a boys' home at 14 years of age. I did have contact with my real family all of my life. From time to time, they visited me while I was in foster care and I was able to see them progress in their lives. I knew that they bought property and cars. I can remember them buying a bike for me once in my life which was the only present that I can ever remember receiving from them. My Mother got well and established a career for herself. She must have had some education because she became a Walgreen's Drug Store Company bookkeeper, traveling the country doing their books. She had a decent income for a Black woman in the fifties, sixties and seventies.

The thing that I give credit to my Grandfather for was that he left the South. Two generations behind him, I received the benefit of his move. Although my young life was a little troubling and I did not have the benefit of the family's advancement, I was raised in an environment that instilled in me that I could advance my own self - if I had confidence in myself and worked hard to accomplish the thing that I wanted. I doubt that I could have gained those confidences and that attitude if I had been born and raised in the Jim Crow South in the nineteen thirties and forties. During that time in the South, Black people were taught to be submissive in their demeanor to White people and to have no uppity ambitions. I was always defiant, even to the extent that it got me in trouble when I was young, but it turned out to be a good characteristic when I got older and I needed it the most.

All the Black men and woman, who left the south after The Civil War, left their future generation in a better position to advance their lives. Although there was bigotry and discrimination in the North of America, it was not as pervasive as it was in the South. Black generation after generation was able to inherit, from Black forefathers that had passed on, boldness, skills and tactics to advance their lives.

After generations of Blacks had passed on, those Blacks that came behind them were not looking in the graves of those that had passed on for future strategies for improvements to their lives. They felt reverence for the memories of and were inspired by those that went before them, but they understood that Death had consumed those generations of men and women who laid in their graves and that those in the graves could do nothing more for them. I think that most cultures in the world feel the same way. Beyond that, I don't think that the majority of mankind, with the exception of some voodoo sects, thinks that dead people can do anything for us or against us. Hollywood and the film industry have made a ton of money using their imagination to bring dead people alive on the screen. Men thought up zombies for entertainment and financial value.

During my search while writing this book, I did not find anything that would lead me to believe that there is any life after death. I did come to the opinion that what is important is what one does while they are living and that while living a person or a generation of persons should understand that what they do in life is important to their own generation and to future generations. My generation solved the problem of space travel. My generation inherited rocket formulas from prior generations which enabled my generation to go to the moon. The present generation is working on galaxies travel which future generation will benefit from.

What you did (do) during your life is important. What you are able to pass on to future men is your heritage.

There is no evidence that a life after death exists that influences man's life. There is a ton of evidence that what one does during life, has a big impact on the present life of man and on the future generations.

Made in the USA
Monee, IL
07 May 2020

30110261R00056